CW00515157

Mollett Victorian B
20 Milestone Chall...ges

Mollett Victorian Bulldog Memorable Moments.
Includes Milestones for Memories, Gifts, Socialization
& Training

Volume 1

Todays Doggy

Copyright © 2019

Dedicated To All of You Wonderful Owners and Fans

Introduction

Welcome to the Original Doggy Milestone Series™ where you are encouraged to create those special moments with your dog. We have composed the milestones in a way that challenges you to set the stage before taking your photos.

Use props and make it fun - be creative in setting up your photos. Get family and friends involved - take it out with you - use it in different places and settings - have a play with it and most importantly, have a good time!

You can either hold the desired milestone spread open yourself - or have somebody hold it open as you take the snap.

If you would like to have the selected milestone book spread open and standing independently in your photos, you can use one or two large 'foldback' clips to hold the spread open.

Good luck and enjoy your photo fun.

I Love My Family...

...And My Family Loves Me

At The
Beach!

Having a Wave of a Time

With My Doggy Pals

IT'S...

BED

TIME

I DIDN'T KNOW WHICH STICK YOU THREW

SO I BOUGHT BACK ALL OF THEM

They Say
Diamonds
Are a Girl's
Best Friend

I Disagree! I'm The Only "Best Friend" Here!

I'm Going To Start Eating Healthy...

Next Week!

DO
NOT
DISTURB

PLAYING

IN THE

LEAVES

I Need

a

HUGe

Amount of Treats

Say

ello

To My Little Friend

OFF

To

The

VET??

CATCH ME IF YOU CAN!

KEEP

CALM

WE'RE
A
TEAM

NASA

Wants

To Hire

Me

Because

I'm a

STAR!

OOPS!
I
Buried
Your
Stuff

...But I Forgot Where

Forgot

Where

I'm a Super Hero

My
Real
Name
Is
SUPER
POOCH

Very

Incredible

Pup

I

DIDN'T

DO IT

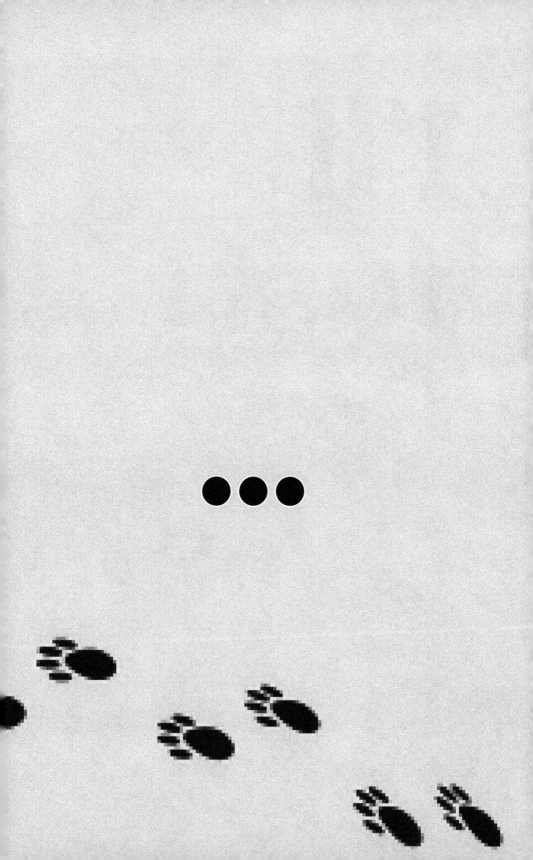

I'll Just Be Over Here...

Looking

Fabulous

PLEASE

PLEASE

PRETTY PLEEEASE

CAN I KEEP IT?

I'm On a SEAFOOD Diet

When
I SEE
FOOD,
I EAT
IT!

CPSIA information can be obtained
at www.ICGtesting.com
Printed in the USA
LVHW081255210819
628164LV00042B/1725/P

9 781395 329808